Let's Talk About Finance for Women

Rev. Stephanie Denise

Table of Contents

Chapter I: The Power of Financial Literacy for Women

In the journey of faith, one of the essential paths we must walk is the path of financial literacy. Wealth and resources are often misunderstood, particularly within the context of our faith. Yet, as we delve into the Scriptures, we find a plethora of guidance that speaks to the importance of taking charge of our financial destinies. This realization is vital, especially for women, who have historically been relegated to the sidelines when it comes to money management.

Understanding Financial Literacy

Financial literacy is not merely about understanding money; it's about empowerment. It is the knowledge and skills necessary to manage financial resources effectively for a lifetime of financial well-being. Proverbs 31:16 tells us, "She considers a field and buys it; with the fruit of her hands she plants a vineyard." This verse exemplifies the wisdom and foresight women possess when they actively engage with their finances.

As women, we need to embrace this same mindset. It's not just a matter of income; it's about stewardship. We are stewards of what God has entrusted to us. Ignorance in financial matters can lead to mismanaged resources, anxiety, and a sense of powerlessness. Therefore, taking control of our finances is not just a matter of dollars and cents, but a vital aspect of fulfilling our God-given purpose.

Why Women Need to Take Control of Their Finances

Empowerment: Knowing how to manage our finances gives us the confidence to make informed decisions. When we educate ourselves about budgeting, saving, and investing, we enable ourselves to live not just for today but to build towards tomorrow.

Responsibility: Proverbs 27:23 reminds us, "Be thou diligent to know the state of thy flocks and look well to thy herds." We must take responsibility for our financial well-being. God has given us the ability to manage resources, and it is our duty to exercise that stewardship.

Independence: Financial independence means freedom. It allows us to pursue God's calling without being overly reliant on others for financial stability. This independence empowers us to support not just ourselves but also our families and communities.

Generational Impact: Our financial behaviors and knowledge can reflect on future generations. By taking control of our finances, we set a powerful example for our children. Deuteronomy 6:6-7 tells us to teach our children diligently. This includes not just spiritual teachings but practical lessons on handling money.

Security: Financial literacy provides a safety net in times of uncertainty. Life is unpredictable; however, having a handle on our finances allows us to weather storms and remain steadfast.

Five Actions Women Can Take Today to Care for Their Finances

Create a Budget: Start by writing down your income and expenses. Identify areas where you can save. Remember, budgeting is about consciously deciding where our money goes. As Proverbs 21:5 states, "The plans of the diligent lead surely to abundance."

Educate Yourself: Read books, attend workshops, or take online courses on financial management. Knowledge is power, and the more you learn, the better decisions you can make.

Open a Savings Account: If you don't already have one, set aside a portion of your income for emergencies or future goals. Proverbs 21:20 reminds us, "There is precious treasure and oil in the dwelling of the wise." Save for your future, for it is a wise choice.

Develop a Debt Repayment Plan: If you have outstanding debts, outline a plan to tackle them head-on. Consider the snowball method, where you pay off the smallest debts first to gain momentum and motivation.

Invest Wisely: Start looking into investment options, even if it's just modest contributions to a retirement account. God desires for us to use our resources wisely, and investing can be a means of multiplying what we have been given. Ecclesiastes 11:2 advises us to "Cast your bread upon the waters, for you will find it after many days."

In Conclusion

As we navigate our financial journeys, let us remember that financial literacy is not just a skill; it is an avenue through which we can express our faith and fulfill our God-given potentials. We have the authority to take control of our finances, which ultimately allows us to exercise dominion in all aspects of our lives. Let us lean on Scripture for wisdom and guidance, and take bold steps into a brighter financial future.

Today, let us all commit to being proactive, enlightened, and faithful stewards of the resources we have been blessed with. And let us always remember, "With God, all things are possible" (Matthew 19:26)—including achieving financial literacy and independence.

Chapter II: Breaking the Silence: Courageously Confronting the Money Taboo

As we walk this journey of faith, it's crucial that we address the often unspoken, yet deeply entrenched taboo around money. Our relationship with finances is woven intricately into our lives, impacting how we view ourselves, our community, and our God-given purpose. It is time for us—especially as women—to speak boldly about money, overcoming the shame that has silenced our voices for far too long.

The Burden of Silence

In my own journey, I've felt the weight of silence when it comes to money discussions. Society often teaches us that talking about finances is impolite, and as women, we've been socialized to diminish our worth, often leading to feelings of shame or inadequacy when it comes to our financial literacy. But let us not forget that God desires us to live abundant lives (John 10:10).

The Bible supports our need for understanding and managing finances wisely. Proverbs 21:5 tells us, "The plans of the diligent lead surely to abundance, but everyone who is hasty comes only to poverty." This scripture invites us to embrace the notion that financial literacy is not merely a skill, but a reflective dance of diligence, intention, and faith.

Overcoming the Shame

Breaking the silence begins with us addressing the shame often associated with our financial situations—whether we are in abundance or lack. It's essential to recognize that our finances do not define our worth as women of God. In 1 Timothy 6:10, we read, "For the love of money is a root of all kinds of evil." The emphasis is not on money itself, but rather the love of it that can lead us astray. When we shift our focus from love of money to stewardship and responsible management, we begin to see money as a tool for God's purposes rather than a source of shame.

Embracing Courage

Courage is fundamental in confronting this taboo. God equips us with the strength to face uncomfortable truths. As we pursue financial literacy, we cultivate resilience and clarity in our purpose. Joshua 1:9 encourages us with the words, "Have I not commanded you? Be strong and courageous. Do not be frightened, and do not be dismayed, for the Lord your God is with you wherever you go." With this promise, we can step forward boldly into the discomfort that financial conversations may create.

Action Steps to Empower Change

To support our journey in breaking the money taboo, I encourage you to take the following steps:

Educate Yourself: Dedicate time to learning about financial literacy. Read books, attend workshops, or take online courses. Equip yourself with knowledge that will empower your understanding and decision-making.

Gather a Support Network: Create or join a group of women who arc open to discussing finances. Share your stories, struggles, and strategies in a safe space. This will help to normalize the conversation around money and build accountability.

Create a Budget: Take a personal inventory of your finances. Create a budget that reflects your values and goals. As you do this, pray over your financial decisions, inviting God into your financial planning.

Shift Your Mindset: Challenge any negative beliefs you hold about money. Journaling can be a powerful tool for this. Write down these beliefs and counter them with God's truth found in Scripture.

Give Generously: Practice generosity with your finances. This doesn't have to be limited to monetary gifts but can include your time and resources as well. Malachi 3:10 encourages us to "bring the full tithe into the storehouse," which can help cultivate a spirit of gratefulness and abundance in our lives.

Conclusion

Breaking the silence around money is not merely about achieving financial stability; it's about stepping into the fullness of life that God desires for us. As women of faith, the act of discussing, managing, and sharing our resources becomes an act of courage and community.

Let us boldly declare, as we do in Philippians 4:19, "And my God will supply every need of yours according to his riches in glory in Christ Jesus." We are not alone in this journey. Together, let's embrace our purpose, empowered by our knowledge and courage, to break free from the bondage of shame and silence surrounding money.

Through faith and action, we can rewrite the narrative around money and become women who thrive financially, spiritually, and purposefully, bringing glory to God in every step of our financial journey.

Chapter III: Transforming Your Money Mindset: Embracing Abundance Through Faith

Sisters, as we embark on this journey together, I want you to reflect on the profound truth that our mindset shapes our reality. When it comes to money, the way we think can either propel us toward abundance or keep us shackled in scarcity. As women of faith, it is essential that we embrace a positive money mindset that aligns with God's promises of provision and abundance.

Understanding Money Mindset

Many of us have grown up with ingrained beliefs about money that may reflect scarcity, fear, or even guilt. Perhaps you've heard phrases like "money is the root of all evil" or "there's never enough to go around." Though these phrases may have come from a place of good intention, they can create a mindset that limits our potential to thrive.

Scripture reminds us in Proverbs 23:7, "For as he thinks in his heart, so is he." This powerful verse tells us that our thoughts dictate our actions, and consequently our outcomes. Therefore, transforming our money mindset from one of scarcity to one of abundance is crucial.

The Abundance of God

God desires for us to experience abundance—not just in our finances, but in every aspect of life. John 10:10 assures us, "I came that they may have life and have it abundantly." Abundance can manifest through peace, joy, and plenty. When we adopt a mindset of abundance, we begin to see our financial struggles not as roadblocks, but as opportunities to trust in God's provision.

When we focus on God's promises, we can shift from a scarcity mindset focused on what we lack to a mindset grounded in gratitude for what we have. Philippians 4:19 assures us, "And my God will supply every need of yours according to his riches in glory in Christ Jesus." This assurance frees us from fear, empowering us to claim our inheritance as children of the King.

Five Action Steps to Shift Your Money Mindset

Now that we've laid the foundation, let's dive into practical steps you can take right away to explore and shift your money mindset:

Reflect on Your Money Beliefs: Take time to write down any beliefs you currently hold about money. Are they positive or negative? What assumptions have you inherited from your family or culture? Bring these beliefs before God in prayer, asking for His guidance to reveal the truth about your financial situation.

Practice Gratitude: Shift your focus from what you don't have to what God has already provided. Begin a gratitude journal dedicated to your financial blessings. Each day, jot down at least three things you're thankful for regarding your finances. This practice will help reinforce a mindset of abundance.

Affirm Abundance: Incorporate positive affirmations into your daily routine. Speak aloud statements such as, "I am a steward of God's blessings" or "Money flows to me effortlessly and abundantly." Let these affirmations reshape your thoughts and align them with God's promises.

Educate Yourself: Knowledge is power, and in the context of finances, it can be transformational. Read books or take courses on financial literacy. Equip yourself with tools to manage your money wisely. The more informed you are, the more confident you will feel in managing your finances.

Create a Vision Board: Visualize your goals by creating a vision board that reflects your financial aspirations and dreams. Whether it's owning a home, starting a business, or becoming debt-free, place images and words that inspire you. Hang it where you can see it daily, reminding yourself that abundance is within reach.

Embracing the Journey

As we embark on this journey to reshape our money mindset, remember that it's a process. Just as it took time for negative thoughts to take root, it will require intentionality and patience to cultivate new, positive beliefs. Surround yourself with supportive individuals who uplift and encourage you, for "Iron sharpens iron, and one man sharpens another" (Proverbs 27:17).

Sisters, let us lean into God's promises, recognizing that as we shift our mindset to one that embraces abundance, we can step boldly into our purpose and calling. The spirit of abundance will open doors we never thought possible, guiding us toward fulfillment in our financial lives and beyond.

In everything you do, trusted sister, remember the words of 2 Corinthians 9:8: "And God is able to make all grace abound to you, so that having all sufficiency in all things at all times, you may abound in every good work."

God is calling us to a life of abundance that reflects His glory. Let us grab hold of this opportunity to shift our money mindset and walk in faith toward the abundance that God so graciously provides.

Chapter IV: Making Money Work for You: A Journey of Faith and Wealth

As we embark on this journey together, let us remember that our financial stewardship is not just about accumulating wealth for ourselves, but about creating a legacy for our children and future generations. In Proverbs 13:22, we are reminded, "A good person leaves an inheritance for their children's children." This scripture resonates deeply within the hearts of those who understand that wealth is a tool for empowerment, not an end in itself.

Understanding Wealth Through Faith

Wealth is often viewed through the lens of materialism, but as women of faith, we know that true wealth transcends the physical. It encompasses our spiritual, emotional, and financial well-being. God has entrusted us with resources, and it is our responsibility to manage them wisely. This chapter will guide you through practical strategies for investing and planning for the future, ensuring that your financial decisions align with your faith and values.

Strategies for Investing

1. Educate Yourself:

Knowledge is power. Start by learning the basics of investing. Books, online courses, and financial workshops can provide you with the tools you need to make informed decisions. Remember, Proverbs 4:7 tells us, "The beginning of wisdom is this: Get wisdom. Though it cost all you have, get understanding."

2. Create a Budget:

Establishing a budget is the first step in taking control of your finances. Track your income and expenses, and identify areas where you can save. This discipline will free up resources for investing.

3. Start Small:

You don't need a fortune to begin investing. Consider starting with a small amount in a retirement account or a low-cost index fund. The key is to start somewhere, as even small investments can grow significantly over time.

Building Personal and Generational Wealth

Wealth building is a marathon, not a sprint. It requires patience, perseverance, and a well-thought-out plan. Here are three action steps to take today that will set you on the path toward financial freedom:

Short-Term Action Steps

1. Set Clear Financial Goals:

Write down your short-term and long-term financial goals. Whether it's saving for a vacation, paying off debt, or investing for retirement, clarity will keep you focused and motivated.

2. Open a Savings Account:

If you haven't already, open a high-yield savings account to start saving for your goals. Aim to save at least three to six months' worth of expenses for emergencies.

3. Network with Like-Minded Women:

Surround yourself with women who are also on a journey to financial empowerment. Join a local investment club or an online community where you can share insights, encouragement, and resources.

Long-Term Action Steps

1. Invest in Retirement Accounts:

If your employer offers a 401(k) plan, take advantage of it, especially if they match contributions. If not, consider opening an IRA. The earlier you start, the more your money can grow through compound interest.

2. Diversify Your Investments:

As you become more comfortable with investing, explore different asset classes such as stocks, bonds, and real estate. Diversification can help mitigate risks and increase your chances of building wealth.

3. Create a Legacy Plan:

Begin thinking about how you want to leave a legacy for your children. This may include setting up a trust, investing in their education, or establishing a charitable foundation. As we learn in Proverbs 22:6, "Start children off on the way they should go, and even when they are old they will not turn from it."

Leaving a Legacy

Leaving a legacy goes beyond financial wealth; it includes instilling values, principles, and a strong work ethic in our children. As we build our wealth, let us also focus on teaching our children about money management, the importance of giving, and how to use their resources to serve others.

In closing, remember that making money work for you is a journey of faith, wisdom, and intentionality. Embrace the process, trust in God's provision, and take actionable steps toward building a legacy of wealth that honors Him and blesses future generations.

As you step into this new chapter of financial empowerment, hold on to the promise found in Philippians 4:19: "And my God will meet all your needs according to the riches of his glory in Christ Jesus." Trust that as you seek His kingdom first, He will guide your financial decisions and provide for your every need.

Now, Sisters let's take these steps together, with faith as our foundation and purpose as our guide. Your journey to wealth begins today!

Conclusion:

Embracing Your Journey to Wealth and Legacy

Dear Sisters in Faith,

As we conclude our enlightening journey through the chapters of wealth building and legacy creation, I am filled with gratitude for the time we have shared and the insights we have gleaned together. Each chapter has been a stepping stone, guiding us toward a deeper understanding of our financial empowerment as women of faith. We have uncovered not only the principles of financial stewardship but also the divine calling to leave a lasting legacy for our families and communities.

In our first chapter, we established that our relationship with money transcends mere transactions; it is a sacred journey intertwined with our spiritual growth. We embraced the truth found in Jeremiah 29:11, which reassures us of God's plans for our prosperity. This understanding shifts our perspective, allowing us to see our financial aspirations as part of a greater divine purpose.

As we ventured into the second chapter, we recognized the importance of investing in ourselves. We discovered that education, personal development, and the pursuit of wisdom are essential components of our wealth-building strategy. Proverbs 4:7 reminds us that wisdom is paramount, and as we seek knowledge, we empower ourselves to make choices that lead to financial freedom and fulfillment.

In our third chapter, we took actionable steps toward financial planning and investment. We learned the significance of budgeting, saving, and making informed investments. The wisdom of Luke 14:28 encouraged us to plan with intention, ensuring that we lay a solid foundation for our financial endeavors. Each decision we make today paves the way for a brighter tomorrow.

Finally, in our last chapter, we delved into the profound responsibility of leaving a legacy. We are not merely accumulating wealth for ourselves; we are building a future for our children and generations yet unborn. Psalm 112:1-3 beautifully encapsulates the blessings that come from living a life of faith and righteousness. Let us strive to be women whose legacy is marked by faith, wisdom, and abundance.

As we step forward from this journey, I urge you to take these three vital action steps:

1. Reflect and Pray:

Spend time in prayer, seeking God's guidance on your financial journey. Allow Him to illuminate areas for growth and provide wisdom in your decision-making.

2. Create a Vision Board:

Visualize your financial goals and the legacy you wish to leave. Collect images, scriptures, and quotes that inspire you, and create a vision board to serve as a daily reminder of your aspirations.

3. Start a Savings Plan:

Begin setting aside money for your future, no matter how small the amount. Consider opening a high-yield savings account or starting an investment account to cultivate your wealth over time.

Remember, sisters, that this journey is not a sprint but a marathon. Each step you take, however small, brings you closer to the abundant life God has promised you. Embrace the process, trust in God's timing, and know that you are not alone.

Together, we can build a legacy that reflects our faith and empowers future generations.

May your journey be filled with blessings, wisdom, and the courage to pursue the dreams God has placed in your heart. With love and faith, let us rise together to embrace the wealth and legacy awaiting us.

In His Grace,

Reverend Stephanie Denise

Rev Stephanie Denise is a Twin Mom, Teacher, Author, and Real Estate Investor.

Financial Literacy and Wealth building is key for generational legacy and foundational. Take time to build a wealth mindset and embody a holistic approach to wealth that includes personal well-being and a sense of fulfillment.

Mission: Finding Purpose Within.

Having a purpose allows us to look forward towards a goal instead of looking back to the past. With Purpose our focus looks beyond the day, beyond next week, beyond next month, and even beyond next year. Purpose enables us to get past the not so good days and keep moving forward to achieve our divine purpose filled with love, light, and creativity. Purpose ignites imagination which brings in every part of you; your mind , your heart and your soul. Walking in Purpose is exciting and invigorating! Let's find your Purpose Within.

Vision Statement: "To inspire and support individuals navigating life as empty nesters, while sharing practical wisdom and wealth building tips."

Education:

- Bachelor of Arts in Liberal Arts and Minor in African American Studies, California State University, Hayward, 1997

- Multiple Subject Teaching Credential (K-12), 1998

- Master of Divinity, Pacific School of Religion, 2003

- Doctor of Ministry Studies, Berkeley School of Theology, course work complete, dissertation pending: 2019-Present

www.linkedin.com/in/stephanie-clark-774040188
www.revstephaniedenise.com
revstephaniedenise71@gmail
 @ReverendStephanieDenise
 @StephanieClark-71

Made in the USA
Las Vegas, NV
22 November 2024

12328658R00016